First published in Great Britain in 2009 by
Frances Lincoln Children's Books, 4 Torriano Mews,
Torriano Avenue, London NW5 2RZ
www.franceslincoln.com

British Library Cataloguing in Publication Data
available on request

ISBN: 978-1-84507-131-8

Illustrated with pastels

Set in Angie

Printed in Singapore
9 8 7 6 5 4 3 2 1

Queen Esther

Jenny Koralek

Illustrated by
Grizelda Holderness

F

FRANCES LINCOLN
CHILDREN'S BOOKS

There was once a rich and powerful King who ruled over the land of Persia. Ahasuerus was his name. He was a fierce soldier, but he also loved to hold great feasts and to walk in his beautiful gardens, which were famous throughout the whole wide world.

One day the King decided he must have a wife.
He sent for all the young girls in his vast kingdom
and chose the most beautiful one.
Her name was Esther.

Esther was an orphan living with her cousin, Mordecai.
Their family was from Jerusalem, and Mordecai loved Esther
as if she was his own daughter. He served the King faithfully.
But he was not happy when the King chose Esther to be his wife.

"Promise me," Mordecai said, as he kissed her good-bye,
"you won't tell anyone that you are a Jew. Many people at
the palace hate us Jews because we were once their enemies."

"I promise," said Esther, and away she went to get ready for her wedding. Her seven maids bathed her in precious, sweet-smelling oils and brushed her hair until it shone.

When Esther appeared before the King dressed as a bride, he crowned her with a golden crown. He ordered a holiday for everyone, and gave gold coins to all the poor people in the city. Then he and Esther sat down with hundreds of guests to a grand wedding feast.

That night, Mordecai overheard two
royal guards plotting to kill the King.
He quickly sent a message to Esther,
she told the King, and the two men
were arrested.

Mordecai had saved the King's life,
and his name was written down in the
King's Book of Records. But the King
soon forgot all about it.

Now, the King's most powerful servant was his Grand Vizier,
Haman. Everyone had to bow low whenever Haman appeared.
But Mordecai never bowed down to him.

"Why don't you bow down to me?" Haman asked Mordecai one day.

"I am a Jew," said Mordecai, "and Jews only bow down to God."

Haman grew angrier and angrier with Mordecai. He decided to get rid of him and all the Jews living in Persia. He sat down and drew lots with his friends to find the best day for killing the Jews.

Then he went to the King and said, "Your Majesty, the Jews do not obey some of your laws. Why don't you get rid of them?"

The King gave his royal ring of command to Haman and said, "Do what you like with them."

When Mordecai heard the terrible news,
he quickly sent a message to Esther:
*Only you can save us now! Go to the King
and beg him to be merciful.*

Esther sent a message back: *Anyone who goes
before the King uninvited will be put to death –
even I, the Queen.*

You must go, Mordecai replied.

Very well, said Esther, *I will go to him. But first,
you and I must fast and pray, to prepare ourselves.*

For three days and three nights Esther
and Mordecai ate and drank nothing.
Mordecai prayed for help.
Esther prayed for courage.

She was very frightened, but she went
to the King, who was sitting on his great
golden throne.

When the King saw her coming before
him uninvited, his face blazed with anger —
and Esther fainted.

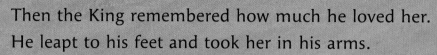

Then the King remembered how much he loved her.
He leapt to his feet and took her in his arms.

"Esther! Esther!" he cried. "What is the matter? It must be
something very important, for you to come to me uninvited."

"O great King!" said Esther, "I have just one favour to ask.
Please be my guest tomorrow at a special dinner, and bring
Haman with you."

The King agreed.

Haman was delighted, and rushed home to tell his wife.

"Guess what? I have been invited to dine with the King and Queen! That will show everyone just how important I am. O happy day! The only thing spoiling it is that wretched Mordecai who refuses to bow down to me. What can I do about him?"

"Have a gallows built," said his wife, "and ask the King to have Mordecai hanged."

Haman thought that was a good idea, and had a gallows built.

That night the King could not sleep a wink. So he sent for his Book of Records and had it read to him. When he heard how Mordecai had once saved his life, he asked, "And what was his reward?"

"There was no reward, Your Majesty," came the answer.

Early next morning Haman
came in, hoping to get the King's
permission to hang Mordecai.

"Ah, Haman!" cried the King,
"Tell me, how can I reward a man
who has served me well?"

Ah, thought Haman, *he's talking
about me.*

"Your Majesty," he replied, "dress
him in royal robes, put him on the
King's favourite horse and lead him
through the city among the cheering
crowds."

"What a good idea!" cried the King. "Go and find Mordecai.
See that he is dressed in splendid clothes and mounted
on a fine horse, and you yourself shall lead him
through the streets! And be sure to call out
as you go, 'This good man saved
the King's life.'"

Haman had to obey, but deep down
he felt bitter and ashamed.

That evening, after dinner, the King said to Esther,
"And now, my Queen, what can I do to please you?
I love you so much, I would give you half my kingdom."
    Esther took a deep breath. "No, Your Majesty,"
she replied, "that is not what I want." She paused.
    "Go on," said the King. "You know I would give
you anything."

"Your Majesty!" Esther replied. "I want something far more precious. I want the lives of my people. You see, I am a Jew, and we are all going to be killed!"

"By whose order?" asked the King angrily. "Who would do such a terrible thing?"

"The man sitting beside you, Your Majesty," said Esther. "Haman."

The King was horrified. "Take him away
and execute him," he commanded – and Haman
was hanged on the gallows he had built for Mordecai.

Then the King sent for Mordecai. "You shall be my Grand Vizier," he said. And the first thing Mordecai did was tear up Haman's order to kill the Jews.

From that day on, they were treated like everyone else in Persia.

The Jews danced and sang with joy. And to this day
a noisy, happy feast, the Feast of Purim, is held
every year to remember how Queen Esther
saved the lives of her people.